My Divali

Monica Hughes

Raintree

Chicago, Illinois

© 2004 Raintree
Published by Raintree, a division of Reed Elsevier, Inc.
Chicago, Illinois
Customer Service 888-363-4266
Visit our website at www.raintreelibrary.com

Printed and bound in the United States at Lake Book Manufacturing, Inc.
07 06 05 04 03
10 9 8 7 6 5 4 3 2 1

Library of Congress Cataloging-in-Publication Data:
Hughes, Monica.
  My Divali / Monica Hughes.
      p. cm. -- (Festivals)
Summary: Illustrations and simple text describe how one family
celebrates Divali.
Includes bibliographical references and index.
  ISBN 1-4109-0637-X (library binding) -- ISBN 1-4109-0663-9 (pbk.)
  1. Divali--Juvenile literature. 2. Fasts and
feasts--Hinduism--Juvenile literature. 3. Fasts and
feasts--India--Juvenile literature. 4. Hinduism--Customs and
practices--Juvenile literature. [1. Divali. 2. Fasts and
feasts--Hinduism. 3. Hinduism--Customs and practices. 4. Holidays.] I.
Title. II. Series: Hughes, Monica. Festivals.
  BL1239.82.D58H84 2003
  294.5'36--dc22
                        2003010852

Acknowledgments
The Publishers would like to thank Chris Schwarz for permission to reproduce the photographs.

Cover photograph of the children making things at school reproduced with permission of Chris Schwarz.

Every effort has been made to contact copyright holders of any material reproduced in this book.
Any omissions will be rectified in subsequent printings if notice is given to the publishers.

Some words are shown in bold, **like this.** You can find out
what they mean by looking in the glossary on page 24.

Contents

Getting Ready for Divali

Divali is the **Hindu** festival of lights.

My family makes **barfi** for Divali.

We listen to the story of **Rama** and **Sita**.

At School

Our class is making **Divali** decorations.

We act out the story of **Rama** and **Sita.**

Our Shrine

This is my family's shrine.

Lakshmi

Our family makes **puja** to Lakshmi.

Divali Lights

Divali means "row of lights."

I help Dad light little lamps called **diyas.**

There are lots of diyas at this big **shrine**.

At the Mandir

Everyone goes to the **mandir**.

We worship at the **shrines**.

Then, we have fireworks outside.

Divali Sweets

We eat special sweets at **Divali**.

There are **barfi**, **cham chams**, and **ladoos**.

Dressing Up

Mom makes **mehndi** designs. They make my hands look pretty.

We put on new jewelry, too.

Family and Friends

We are going to have a **Divali** party.

18

All of our family and friends
will eat a special meal.

Divali Fun

Inside, we play games and eat sweets.

Outside, we watch dancing and fireworks.

Divali Presents

We get presents for **Divali.**

Mom gives Grandma a present, too.

Happy Divali!

Glossary

barfi sweet made from coconut

cham cham sweet made from milk

Divali New Year festival celebrated by Hindu people in October or November

diya small oil lamp or candle that is used at Divali. Some people call these divas.

Hindu a religion in which people worship many gods and goddesses

ladoo sweet made from milk

Lakshmi Hindu goddess of wealth

mandir place where Hindus go to worship their gods with other Hindus

mehndi designs drawn on women's hands and feet with a special dye called henna

puja honoring or worshiping a god or goddess

Rama and Sita legendary prince and princess who lived more than 2,000 years ago

shrine special place where people honor and worship a god or goddess

Index